YOU CAN TEACH YOURSELF® BLUES PIANO

by Uri Ayn Rovner

D1217462

FOREWORD

The exciting sound of the "blues", born in America, finds its way into all styles of music heard around the world. These days everyone hears that familiar "color" in rock, pop, folk, classical, and other jazz styles. This book shows you what makes the blues unique.

You'll be creating your own music on the piano from this easy-to-follow and complete programmed course. Explanations and examples are given at different levels so you can go over a special section more than once and become even more advanced.

This book works more easily for you when you already know a little about reading piano music. (Also in this series check out *You Can Teach Yourself Piano*.) Playing the blues teaches you essential music theory in a fun "hands-on" way, so a piano teacher can include this as part of your lesson.

All the elements of the basic blues are here. This is a guide, a textbook, and a teacher. If you study music and want to know how to play the blues style, you've come to the right place! Now *You Can Teach Yourself Blues Piano*.

CD CONTENTS

1	Introduction [1:30]	
2	Page 14 [:31]	
3	"C-Saw [:34]	
4	Waltz Of "D-Light" [:19]	
5	"You're The One" [:38]	
6	"All's Well That Ends Well" [:36]	
7	"Ship Shape" [:38]	
8	"A Dozen To Go" [:44]	
9	"Create Your Own 12 Bar" [56]	
10	"Use Your Riff" [1:30]	
11	"Put That Number On The Wall" [:51]	
12	"Twelve Bar Bop" [:47]	
13	"Tap, Tap, Tap" [:57]	
14	"Dallas Blues" [1:17]	

15	"Frankie & Johnny" [1;29]
16	"Back In The Cabbie" [1:16]
17	"You Got The Color Of Blue" [1:27]
18	"A Poor Man Like Me" [:51]
19	"Hesitating Blues" [:48]
20	"Joe Turner" [1:22]
21	"Inspector Blue" [:46]
22	"Create A Song With 9th Accompaniments" [:51]
23	"Borneo Bay" [1:18]
24	"I'm Thinking Of" [1:40]
25	"Tishomingo Blues" [2:22]
26	"Blues Montgomery" [1:46]
27	"Salutations" [2;06]

A stereo cassette tape (95280C) and compact disc (95280CD) of the music in this book is now available. The publisher strongly recommends the use of these recordings along with the text to insure accuracy of interpretation and ease in learning.

Visit us on the Web at http://www.melbay.com – E-mail us at email@melbay.com

CONTENTS

You Can Teach Yourself Blues Piano cassette or CD may be purchased to accompany this book. Songs and exercises marked " ♫ " are on the recording.

REVIEW OF MUSIC NOTATION

(AND SYMBOLS USED IN THIS BOOK)

THE SEVEN LETTERS OF THE MUSICAL ALPHABET

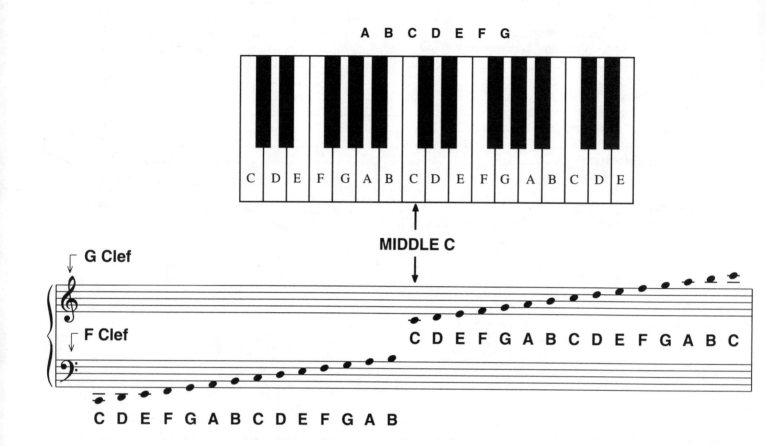

FINGER NUMBERS

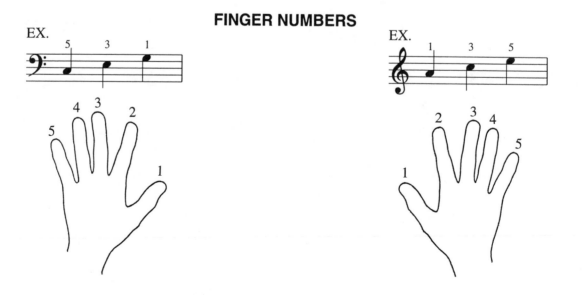

NOTE AND REST VALUES

WHOLE NOTE	HALF NOTES	QUARTER NOTES	EIGHTH NOTES	BAR LINE
4 COUNTS	2 COUNTS EACH	1 COUNT EACH	1/2 COUNT EACH (WRITTEN EITHER WAY)	

WHOLE REST	HALF RESTS	QUARTER RESTS	EIGHTH RESTS	DOUBLE BAR LINE

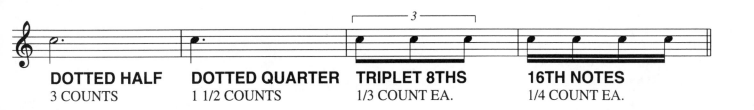

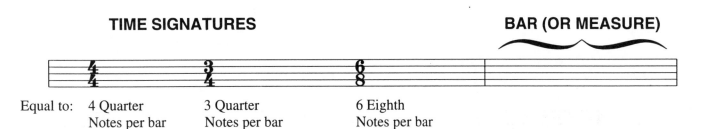

DOTTED HALF	DOTTED QUARTER	TRIPLET 8THS	16TH NOTES
3 COUNTS	1 1/2 COUNTS	1/3 COUNT EA.	1/4 COUNT EA.

Swing

When instructed to swing, eighth notes are not played evenly.
The eighth note on the beat = 2/3 count
The eighth note off the beat = 1/3 count

TIME SIGNATURES   BAR (OR MEASURE)

Equal to: 4 Quarter   3 Quarter   6 Eighth
           Notes per bar   Notes per bar   Notes per bar

OTHER SYMBOLS

ACCENTS
Strike notes harder

STACCATO
Detach notes

SLUR
Connect notes

PLAY: **Softly** **Medium softly** **Medium loudly** **Loudly**

TIE
Add note values together

PLAY NOTE: **FLAT** **SHARP** **NATURAL** **CHORD SYMBOL**
One Chromatic One Chromatic Regular note
Lower Higher

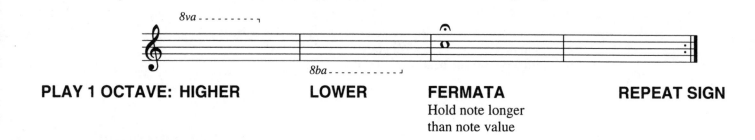

PLAY 1 OCTAVE: HIGHER **LOWER** **FERMATA** **REPEAT SIGN**
Hold note longer
than note value

SUSTAIN
PEDAL GOES: **DOWN** **UP/DOWN** **UP** **DOWN** **UP**

PART ONE

THE MAJOR CHORD

A chord is any three or more notes which go together. The most traditional chord we use is the "major" chord. It has three notes; the **"root"** or the name of the chord, which is its base, the **"third"** of the chord, and the **"fifth"** of the chord.

EXAMPLE:

A chord can start on any note. Each different root note has a different third and fifth. The formula for a major chord is:

      ROOT - Your choice of note

      THIRD - The note 4 half steps (2 steps) higher than the root

      FIFTH - The note 3 half steps (1 1/2 Steps) higher than the third.

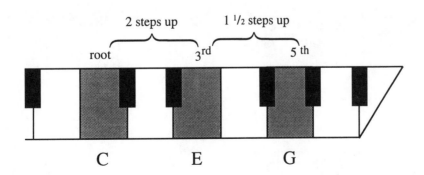

THIS IS A LIST OF MAJOR CHORDS, ONE FOR EACH NOTE

PLAYED

WRITTEN

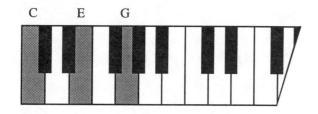

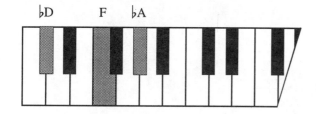

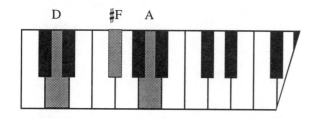

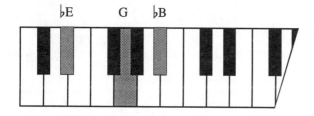

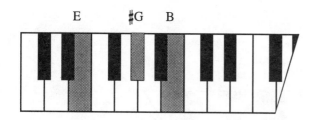

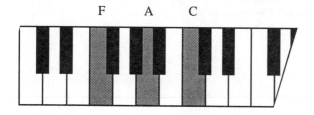

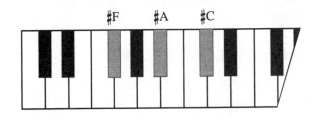

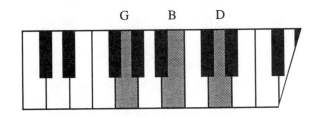

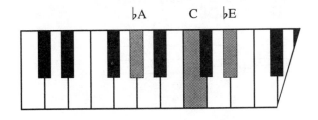

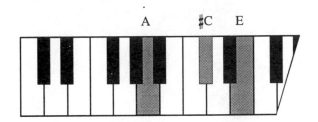

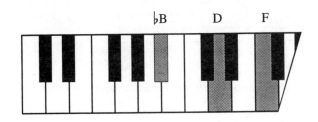

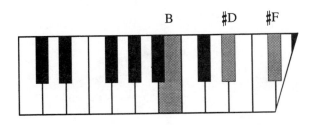

If you want to be able to improvise the blues, you will need to be able to play major chords easily. Let's concentrate on the most important ones first. They fit into three groups.

① THE CHORDS THAT USE ONLY WHITE NOTES:

② THE CHORDS THAT NEED THE "A D E" (AID) OF A BLACK NOTE (A SHARP) IN THE MIDDLE:

③ AND "BUSY B", THE CHORD WITH TWO BLACK NOTES.

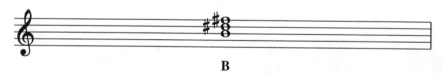

These are the seven chords that have white notes as their root, and the ones we will use most in your first improvisations.

CREATING A SONG WITH CHORDS

Your first song will use a "C" chord explained on the previous pages. The right hand will make up a melody or "tune" while the left hand will play a "blocked" chord. It all starts with the "C" chord....

This is what your hands will look like on their "C" chords:

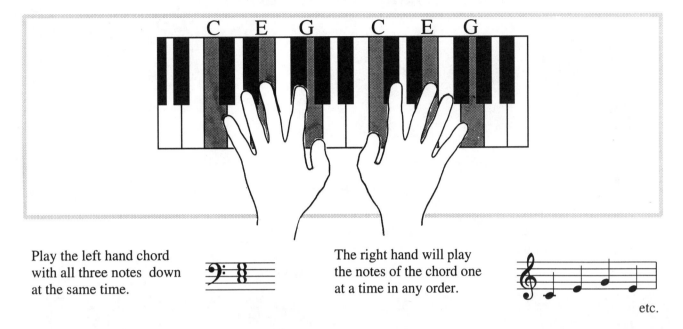

Play the left hand chord with all three notes down at the same time.

The right hand will play the notes of the chord one at a time in any order.

The melody hand can play notes at different lengths, moving up or down the chord or repeating notes, as in the example....

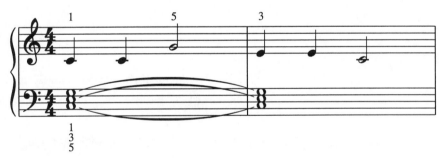

This can be done with any chord the same way; here is the same example on a "D" chord.

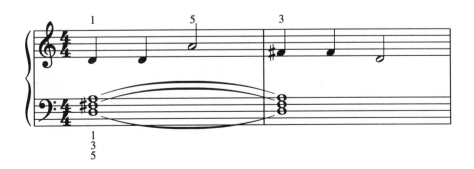

THE "I" AND "V" CHORDS

A song is not complete with only one chord. A complete song has at least 2 different chords. The perfect mate to the **"HOME"** chord, (the chord on which a song is based), is the **DOMINANT** chord. This chord is found at the top of the home chord.

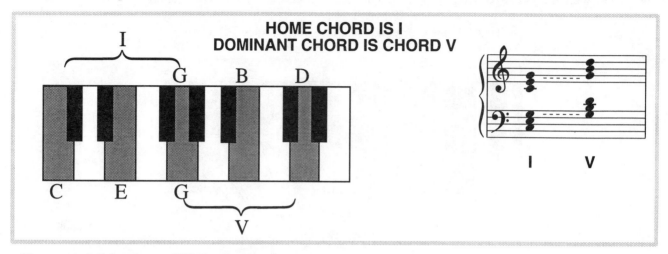

HOME CHORD IS I
DOMINANT CHORD IS CHORD V

Place your left hand on a "C" chord. Now put your pinky where your thumb is, moving your hand to a "G" chord. Go back and forth for the feel.

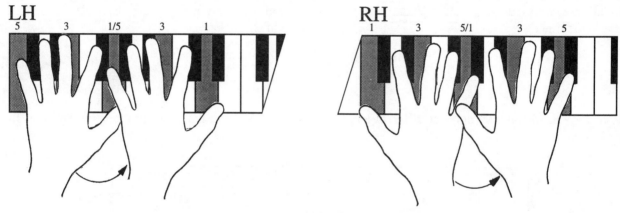

Now place your right hand on a "C" chord. Move up to the "G" chord by putting your thumb where your pinky is.

YOU CAN NOW CREATE A SONG WITH THE FORMULA:
I V I

Play a single note melody above the I chord, then change to the V chord in both hands, continuing the melody. Finish by going back to the I chord. Songs like to end "at home".

Example song in "C"

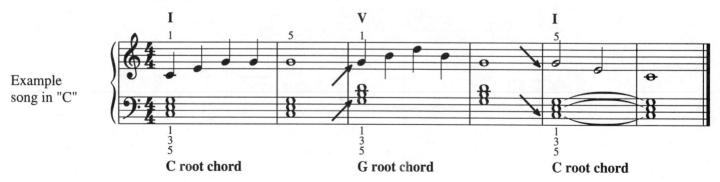

C root chord   G root chord   C root chord

14

"C - SAW"

(IN THE KEY OF C WITH I V I PROGRESSION)

Not too fast

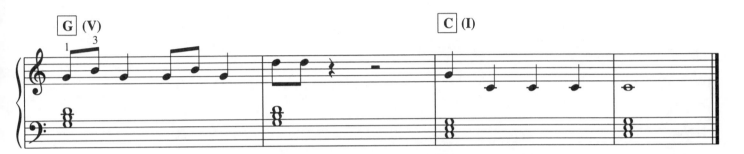

WALTZ OF "D - LIGHT"

(IN THE KEY OF D WITH I V I V I PROGRESSION)

Slowly

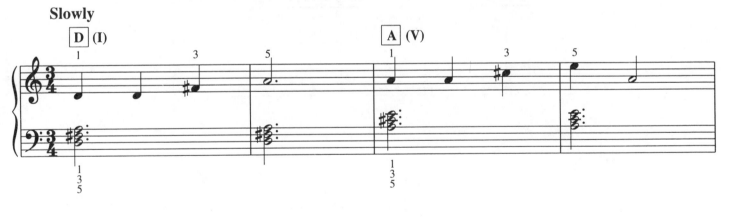

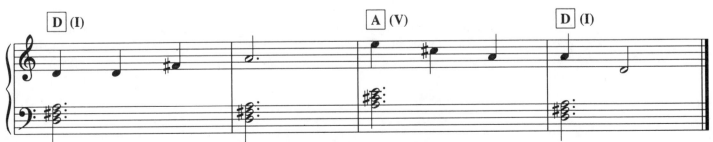

15

YOUR FIRST SONG

It's time to create your own song using two chords. It is in the key of F with the progression I V I. As the first measure shows you, half notes set the pace for the left hand chords. Write in the other left hand measures, then improvise, and write in the right hand melody above it.

TITLE: _____

How you want it played: _____   Your name: _____

A tip about melody making: Keep it simple! A good melody should be easy to sing along with. Try to have very few large leaps up or down, and a good blend of long notes with faster ones. Don't be afraid to use half notes and whole notes, and to repeat some notes.

INTRODUCING THE "IV" CHORD

Just as there are three primary colors, so in music there are **three primary chords.** You are already familiar with the **I** and **V** chords, and now we add the **IV** (four) chord.

The IV chord is actually below the I chord the same distance that the V chord is above the I chord, it is often called "sub-dominant".

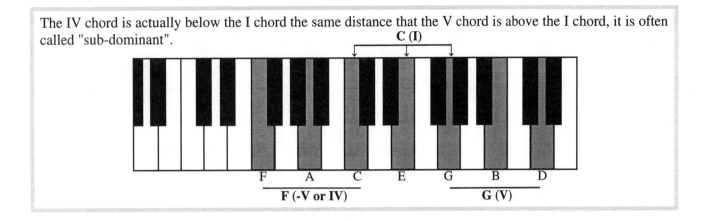

When used in a song along with the I and V chords, it sets up a feeling that the home chord is in the middle, and is now the strongest of the three chords.

Play these three chords several times and listen for which one you think sounds most like "home".

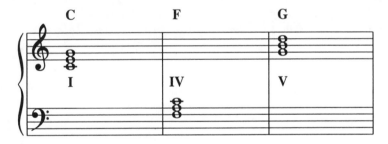

It doesn't matter in which octave you play the IV chord, it will have the same function. The easiest, and fastest way of finding the IV chord is to move **one whole step** **down from the V chord.**

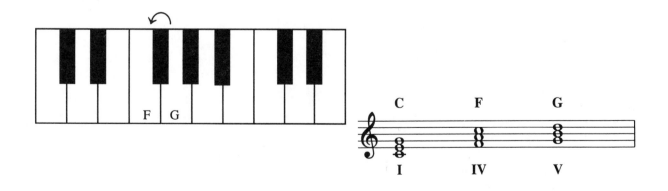

17

THE KEY SIGNATURE

Below is a list of the I, IV, and V chords for all 12 notes. The notes of any I, IV, and V chords combined are called a "key". A key signature is the number of sharps or flats used in a key. If a **key signature** is written at the beginning of a music staff, individual sharps or flats do not need to be written next to those same notes when they occur in the music.

SONGS USING I - IV - V CHORDS

YOU'RE THE ONE

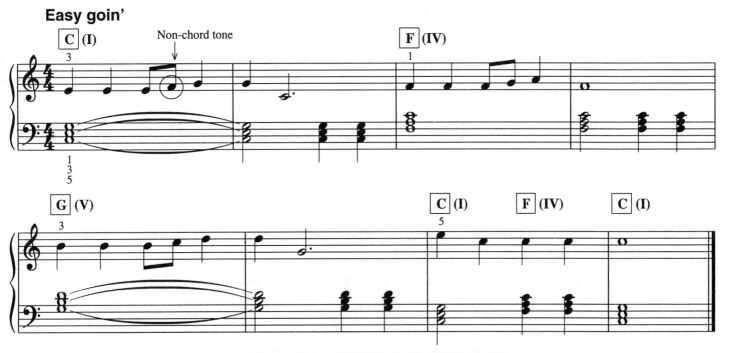

"ALL'S WELL THAT ENDS WELL"

Your help is needed to finish this song! Improvise and write out a tune for the last four measures. The left hand can keep the same chord pattern.

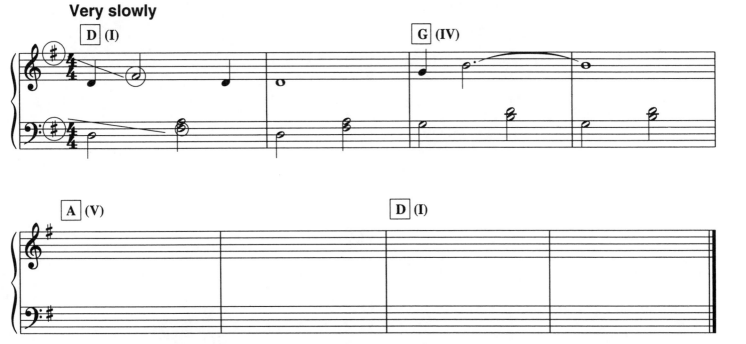

REVIEW OF PART ONE

1. Find the three chords that are all white. Find the three chords that need a sharp in the middle. Which chord is busy?

2. Play all the chords in chromatic order from C chord up to C chord (as on pg. 10-11). Can you play them in 30 seconds or less?

3. Using an F chord, play a chordal melody over a blocked chord in the left hand. Can you turn it around and play the melody in the left hand, and the blocked chord in the right hand?

4. Improvise a five note chordal melody using a C chord. Now transpose that same melody to three other chords.

5. What is the easiest way to find a V chord when you are playing a I chord?

6. What is the easiest way to find a IV chord when you are playing a V chord? Why do we use IV chords?

7. Why are key signatures so helpful?

PART TWO

CHORD INVERSIONS

The chords you have been using for your songs so far have been in root position. This means that the root of the chord is in the bass, (or is the lowest note).

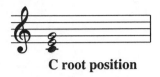

C root position

A chord can have two other positions besides root position. These are called **inversions.** This occurs when the third of the chord is in the bass with the other two notes stacked above. Also when the fifth of the chord is in the bass with the other two notes stacked above.

C 1st inversion

C 2nd inversion

ALL CHORDS HAVE INVERSIONS, HERE ARE SOME EXAMPLES:

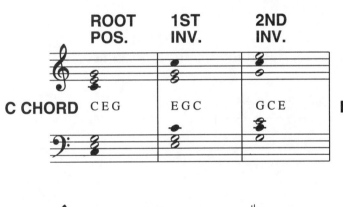

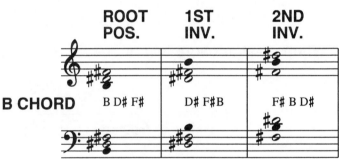

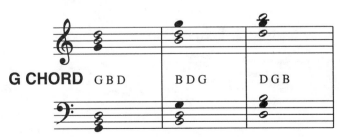

For quick recognition of a chord's name when a chord is in an inversion, always look above the larger space. The large space is the interval of a fourth (two notes skipped). The note just above this large space is the name of the chord. In the examples of the last page you will see them as filled in notes.

Fingering for left hand's first inversion

Fingering for left hand's second inversion

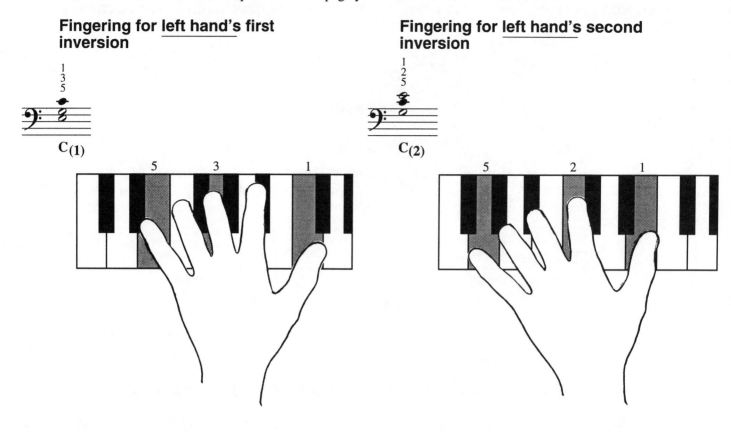

When playing chord inversions for the right hand, the standard fingerings are:

C ROOT   C 1ST INV.   C 2ND INV.

However, use whatever fingering that works best when creating a melody. Sometimes the inversions of a melodic line are mixed, or there are big leaps instead, so you use a fingering that plays the notes easily.

Example 1: C CHORD

Example 2: E CHORD

What fingerings would you use?

USING CHORD INVERSIONS IN A SONG

Prepare for the following song by practicing these inversions for left hand.

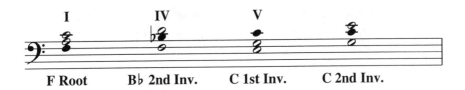

In a right hand melody you can leap to notes out of your handshape, (but in the chord).
Now that you recognize chord notes, or can use your left hand chord notes for a guide,
feel free to move your right hand around to experiment. Notice, for example the melody
of measures 2 and 6 in the following song.

SHIP SHAPE

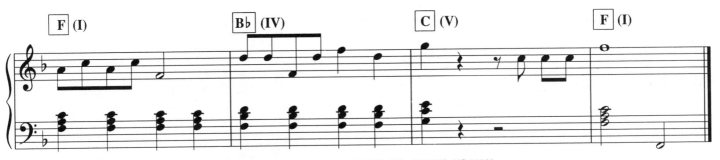

*To swing the rhythm of the melody, play all eighth notes <u>unevenly</u>. All eighth notes that play on the beat
(right on beat 1, 2, 3, or 4) are played longer than the eighth notes off the beat.

THE TWELVE BAR

The blues uses a <u>twelve bar pattern</u> of chords almost exclusively. It means that a song will use the following pattern of <u>twelve measures</u>:

Each measure, usually defined by a **left hand pattern,** must be the same number of beats. The following is an example of a twelve bar. Notice how a left hand pattern can help you count the number of measures you are playing. It is important to memorize this twelve bar pattern of chords:

CREATING A TWELVE BAR SONG

Here are six steps for creating a twelve bar song:

① Decide which key your song will be in.
② Choose a left hand pattern and see how it works for the I, IV, and V chords.
③ Create a four measure long chordal melody for the first line from one of the following:
    A. A two measure idea, with a held note or rest at the end, played twice.
    B. A four measure idea with a held note or rest at the end.
④ Play the same or a similar melody for the second line, (adjust for IV chord.)
⑤ The final four measures of melody can be similar to the others, or different.
⑥ Decide how the song should sound. Should it be fast or slow? Should it
    be loud or soft? Should it swing? In which octave on the keys does it sound best?

Notice how these six steps apply to the following twelve bar......

A DOZEN TO GO

U. A. R.

CREATE YOUR OWN TWELVE BAR

Now you are ready to create your own twelve bar. Follow the steps on page 27. The key and left hand pattern are already given to you.

TITLE: _____

How you want it played: _____   Your name: _____

Can you transpose your song into another key? Just figure out what the three chords will be in the key you choose and play them with the same pattern as above. Next, move your melody notes to fit those chords.

EXTENDING CHORDS WITH A 7TH.

Chords can have more than three notes. The most common chord with four notes is the 7th chord. It is often called a **dominant seventh chord,** but in the blues we use it on any chord, not just the dominant.

There are two ways to find the 7th for a chord:

1.   To a regular three note chord, add the note **one whole step** below the root note. (Be careful of where the root is in a chord inversion!)

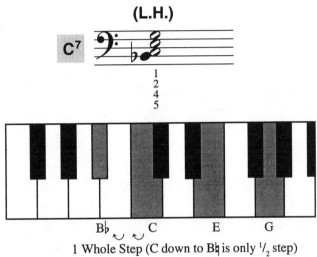

1 Whole Step (C down to B♮ is only ¹/₂ step)

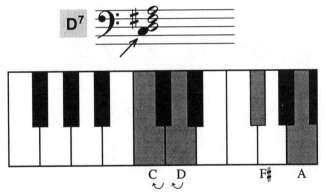

1 Whole Step (D down to D♭ is only ¹/₂ step)

2.   To a root shape chord, add the note **one whole step lower** than the top octave.

29

It is typical of the blues style to put an extended 7th on any chord, whether I, IV, or V, creating I^7, IV^7, or a V^7 chord.

You'll be seeing and playing a lot of these extended chords. The following is a list of the 12 chords with their 7th added in various inversions and shapes.

MELODIC RIFFS WITH SEVENTHS

At this point, to complement the left hand seventh chords, the right hand melody can also include a seventh. In fact, in a twelve bar, the right hand can include a seventh in any melodic **"riff"**, (short musical idea usually repeated to make a musical phrase), even when the left hand does not include one.

Experiment creating some of your own riffs with a seventh. The measures provided below are in $\frac{4}{4}$ time, so be careful to check your rhythm.

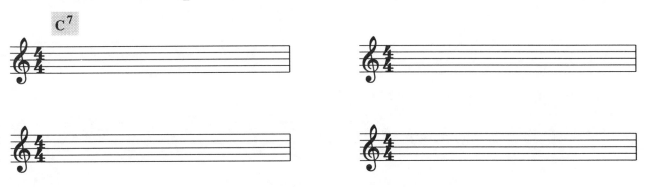

USE YOUR RIFF

In the following twelve bar the left hand pattern has been provided. For the right hand melody, insert one of your riffs with a seventh from page 31. How would this riff sound if it were used the same for each measure? How would you change it to fit the IV and V chords? How can your riff stretch to make a four measure phrase?

(Review the six steps for creating a twelve bar on page 27.)

TITLE: _____

How you'd like it played: _____

Your name: _____

In the following twelve bar you will hear a seventh for each chord in the melody. In both the left hand pattern and the melody are examples of non chord tones, as well. The left hand pattern includes a "sixth", (the third and seventh note of each measure). The melody includes non chord tones to create more steps, like the first three notes. Melodic steps are important, and can be achieved <u>within</u> the chord notes by:

① Using the root note and seventh of a chord next to each other
② Moving up or down one note in the melody as chords change

PUT THAT NUMBER ON THE WALL
(AND GIVE THAT MAN A CALL)

Real slow swing

U. A. R.

Put that num-ber on the wall, and give that man a call.

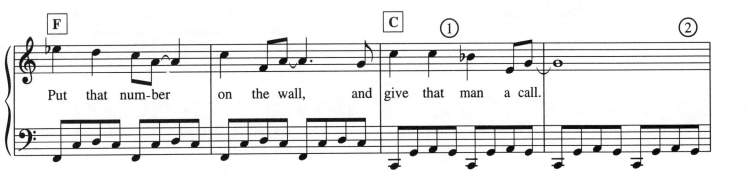

Put that num-ber on the wall, and give that man a call.

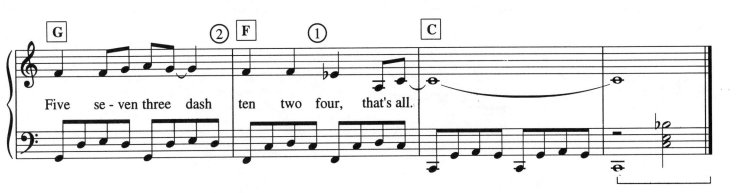

Five se - ven three dash ten two four, that's all.

ACCOMPANIMENT PATTERNS

These are some of the most common left hand patterns for twelve bar. Choose from this list when creating your songs. When you discover other patterns, add them to the list.

* Any eighth note patterns can swing

Some new elements have been added to this twelve bar. It is 24 measures long. This is because each bar has been stretched to two measures in length. So everything is doubled. The melody has been joined by other notes in the right hand creating some **harmony.** This harmony includes some non chordal tones such as the passing tones "D" and "D#" in measure two.

Don't forget to swing!

TWELVE BAR BOP

With energy

U. A. R.

REVIEW OF PART TWO

1. How many inversions can a root chord have?

2. What's a quick way to find the name of a written or played inversion?

3. What's the progression of a twelve bar?

4. Can you show two ways of making a seventh chord? Which hand, the left hand pattern or the melody hand, can have a seventh in it?

5. Can all three lines of a twelve bar be a similar melody?

6. What is the difference between a riff and a melody?

7. Play five different left hand patterns from pages 34 and 35 in a different key. Include I, IV, and V chords.

PART THREE

BLUE NOTES

In the early years of the blues a characteristic that helped define its style was the use of **"blue notes"**. Traditionally a singer or guitar player would start the third, or sometimes the fifth of a chord a half step lower and slide up to the chordal note. This characteristic bending of the melody note can be imitated on the keyboard in any of the following ways:

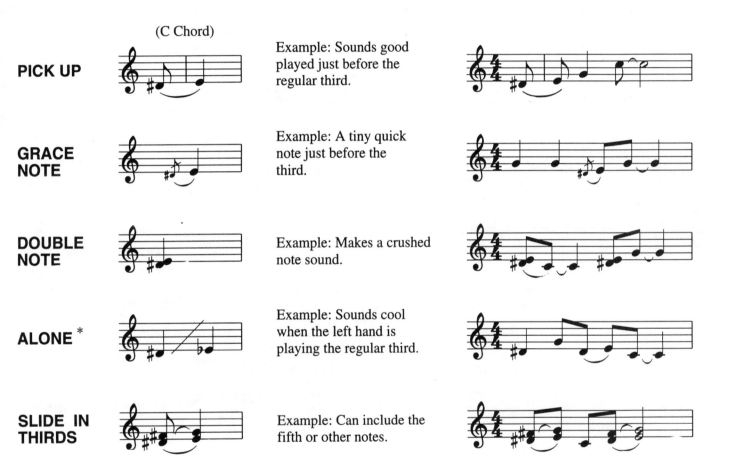

PICK UP — (C Chord)
Example: Sounds good played just before the regular third.

GRACE NOTE
Example: A tiny quick note just before the third.

DOUBLE NOTE
Example: Makes a crushed note sound.

ALONE *
Example: Sounds cool when the left hand is playing the regular third.

SLIDE IN THIRDS
Example: Can include the fifth or other notes.

* The **enharmonic** note E♭ may be used instead of D♯. This is usually done when the note to follow descends stepwise to a "D", for example.

MELODY CHECK

Now that your level of playing the blues has advanced let's check up on melody making. You have a strong foundation of form and structure in your twelve bar, with lots of different patterns for your left hand. Sometimes creating a good melodic line can be the most challenging part.

> * **In what key is this song? What chords are used?**
> * **Can you tell which notes are melody, and which are harmony?**
> * **Are blue notes used? 7ths?**
> * **How was the riff used when the chords change?**
> * **Are other melodic ideas used?**
>
> **Notice how the riff in measure one repeats or expands to create the melody.**

TAP TAP TAP

* **A little lazy like**

U. A. R.

* Although written as a dotted eighth and sixteenth, play just like the regular swing explained on page 25.

"FAKE" A TWELVE BAR

The challenge of this twelve bar is to use the riff below as the basis of a melody. Using the chords given, select a left hand pattern that goes well with the melody you've created, and "fake" the left hand throughout.

MELODIC RIFF:

TITLE: _____

How you want it played: _____   Your name: _____

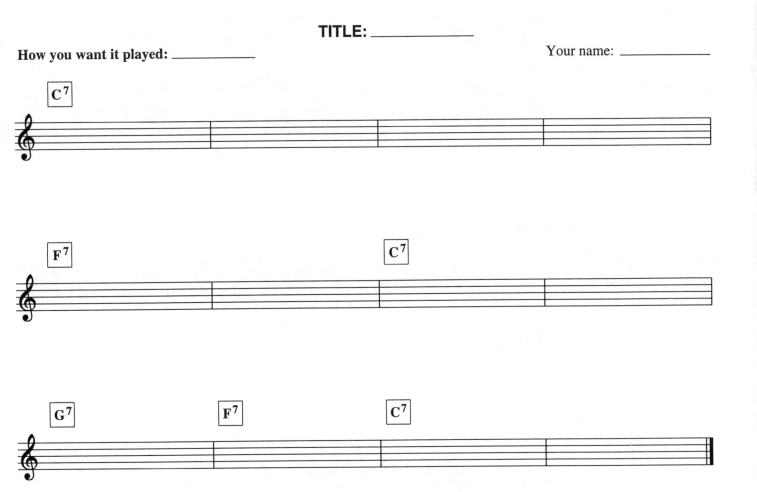

DALLAS BLUES

Swing
Tempo di blues (very slowly)

Hart A. Wand
Arr: U. A. R.

ANALYSIS OF THE DALLAS BLUES MELODY

Here is a step by step analysis of the melody found in the preceding song. Careful attention to how melodies like this are formed may help you create better melodies for your own songs. The top notes of the right hand are the actual melody, with the lower part acting as harmony. Both parts are discussed for this analysis.

MEAS. 1 - 4 .... This is a four measure introduction to the song. These measures set the rhythm, key, and mood for the twelve bar that follows it. The last four measures of the song are used for this intro. More about intros will be discussed in part 4.

MEAS. 5 - 8 ... This is the first line of the first twelve bar. (There are two complete twelve bars for this song). It is a four measure phrase made up of a two measure idea (A), and a two measure idea (B). Note the traditional hold note at the end.

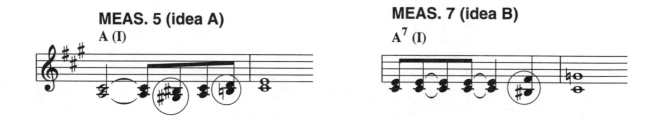

MEAS. 5 (idea A)
A (I)

MEAS. 7 (idea B)
A⁷ (I)

Both **ideas** contain non chord tones. In idea "A" the B♯ is the blue note for the "A" chord. The double note "B + D" are passing notes from one set of notes in the chord to the other. Can you explain the non chord tones in **idea** "B" ?

46

MEAS. 9 - 12 ..... The second line of the twelve bar is different than the first, but it contains the rhythm of idea "B" for the IV chord measures.

IDEA "B" RHYTHM   **MEAS. 9   D⁷(IV)**

MEAS. 13 - 16 ... The last line (of this first twelve bar) is different than the traditional V IV I I pattern we're used to seeing. It is V V I I instead.

Because another complete twelve bar is about to follow, a turnaround, or bridge is found in measure 16 on beats 2 - 3 - 4. The notes step chromatically down to the beginning of M. 17. Turnarounds are discussed in part 4.

TURNAROUND

MEAS. 17 - 20 ... This twelve bar is different than the other. The first line seems to be a four measure phrase with the traditional hold note for the last part. Notice the hold note in the last measure of this first line is the seventh.

The chord structure for this first line is a variation of the usual I I I I. Instead we hear I V I I.

MEAS. 21 - 24 ... The second line is similar to the first line using the same rhythm, and the same four measure phrase format. Note the non chord tones and blue notes.

MEAS. 25 - 28 ... The last line of this twelve bar is the same as the last line of the first twelve bar, and the same as the intro.

Which of these two songs have a melody created from a two measure idea? Which from a four measure idea? Are the lines similar within the twelve bars?

Which left hand pattern would you choose for each song?

FRANKIE AND JOHNNY

Traditional

Fran-kie and John - ny were lov - ers, __ Oh Lord - y how __ they could love.

swore to be true __ to each oth - er, __ true as the stars a - bove. He was her

man, _____ but he done her wrong. _____

BACK IN THE CABBIE

U. A. R.

Back in the cab - bie __ rest - in' my head a - way. _____

Back in the cab - bie __ rest - in' my head a - way. _____

Train go - in' no - where, __ pass my time of day _____

THE BASIC BLUES SCALE FOR "C"

The C blues scale is formed by taking only notes that are found twice among the I IV, and V chords. The chords include a seventh and blue third. There are five notes that do this as shown below:

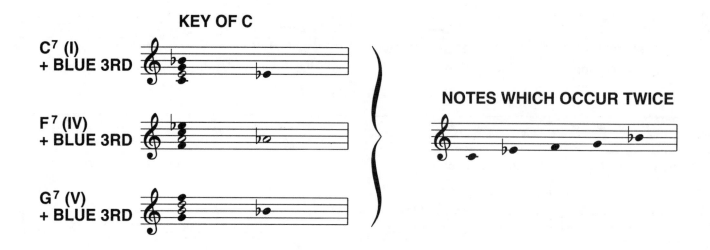

BASIC BLUES SCALE

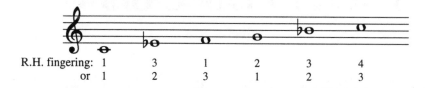

The basic blues scale will be played almost exclusively by the right hand for <u>melody making</u>. The are several fingerings, two are shown. * Notice that the first three and second three notes have a similar pattern.

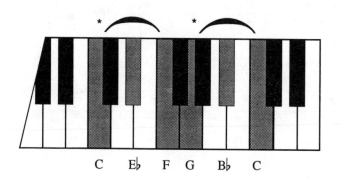

USING THE BLUES SCALE

The design of the blues scale makes it easily used because any of its notes, in any order, can be played over the I, IV, or V chords and sound fine.

Although the melody uses these special notes, the left hand will still use traditional patterns.

Listen to this basic blues scale riff played over each of the I, IV, and V chords for C ...

BLUES RIFF:

PLAYED OVER C⁷ (I)

PLAYED OVER G⁷ (V)

PLAYED OVER F⁷ (IV)

Try your hand at creating a two measure blues riff. Play it over I, IV, and V of your choice of L.H. pattern.

YOUR BLUES RIFF:

In line 3 of a twelve bar blues, the V and IV chord each last only one measure long. If your melodic riff or idea is two measures long, then there are some choices when you get to these measures:

① **Sometimes a two measure blues idea fits just fine over the single V and IV...**

② **It can be fragmented, (use just part of it), repeating it for the second measure...**

③ **Something completely different can be played...**

When we sing the blues, we sing of earthly things; about our trials of everyday life. It's common for the blues to sing about injustice, or depression, or frustration. Sometimes clever poetry lets us laugh at the way we are, or tells a tale of two lovers. Can you think of some words for "You Got The Color Of Blue"?

Just as the notes of the music are often the same for the first and second lines, so the words may be the same too.

YOU GOT THE COLOR OF BLUE

Real slow swing

U. A. R.

Words by: _____

CREATE YOUR OWN BLUES

Compose your own blues twelve bar with the basic blues scale.

You may use your blues riff from page 51 to create your melodic phrase, or create a new one. Left hand patterns are on page 34.

TITLE: _____

How you want it played: _____   Your name: _____

C⁷

F⁷   C⁷

G⁷   F⁷   C⁷

The basic blues scale does not include a half step between any two notes.

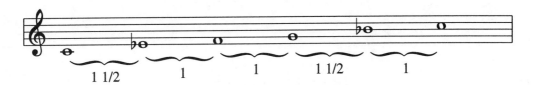

The complete C blues scale adds a G♭. This connects both halves of the basic blues scale and creates two half steps. One between F and G♭, and the other between G♭ and G.

COMPLETE BLUES SCALE:

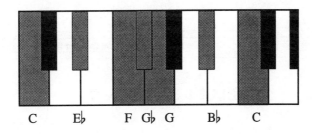

There is no one proper fingering for the blues scale. Different riffs moving up or down the scale will feel better with different fingering than the one suggested here for starters.

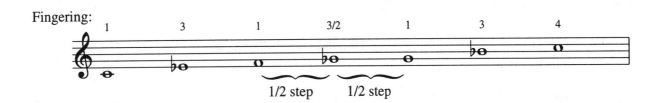

Here are seven different common blues keys with corresponding complete blues scales:

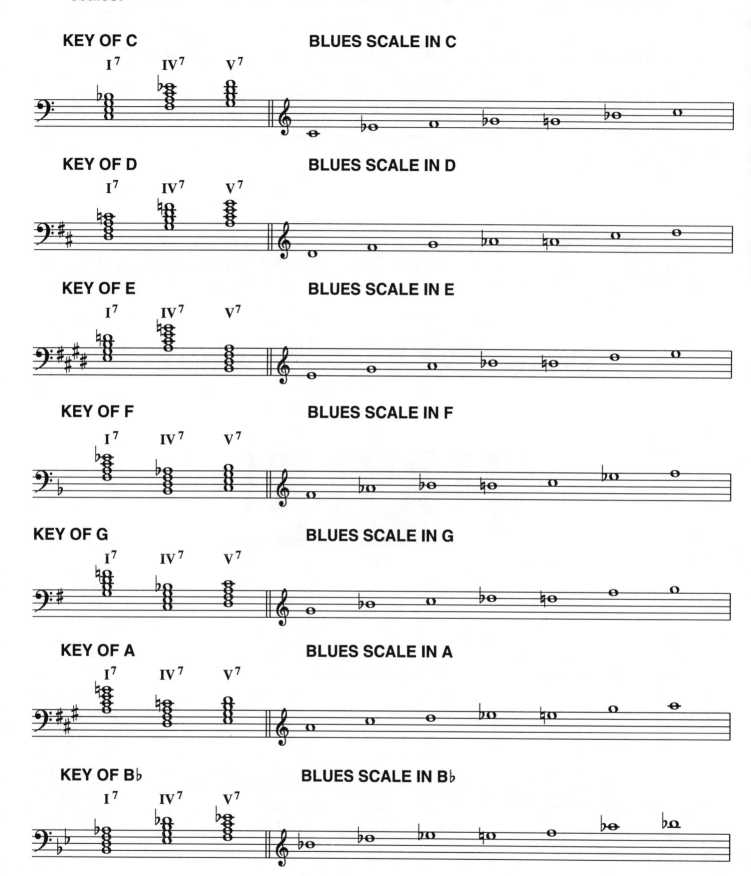

56

The following blues is in the **key of B♭** and uses the **complete blues scale** for its melody. One melody note, however, is chordal and does not fit into the blues scale. Can you find it?

Note how the four measure phrase is used for the first two lines. How is the third line melody related to them?

A POOR MAN LIKE ME

Medium swing

U. A. R.

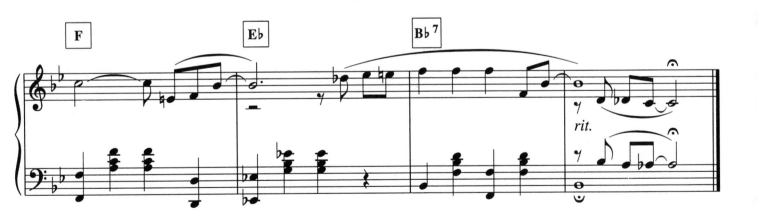

REVIEW OF PART THREE

1. What is a blue note?

2. Which notes would be considered part of a blues "C" chord? ....a blues "D" chord? ......blues "B♭" chord?

3. In which ways can a non chord tone be found in a melody?

4. Where do the notes in a blues scale come from? What is added to a basic blues scale to make it a complete blues scale.

5. Does the blues scale affect mostly the melody hand or the chord hand?

6. Can a riff be designed with just notes from a blues scale?

7. In how many keys can you play a complete blues scale?

8. Is it possible to change the regular pattern of chords in a twelve bar?

PART FOUR

INTRODUCTIONS

A twelve bar blues may begin with an introduction of a few notes or a few measures. It can set the mood of the song before the melody begins. It could also set the tempo and key for a soloist who is about to sing or play.

① **Here is an example of a "pick up", (a few notes leading to beat one.):**

② **In these examples, <u>several measures</u> are given to set the pace. A <u>double bar</u> or <u>repeat</u> sign is often found to separate the intro from the twelve bar.**

③ **EXPANDED INTRO**
This introduction from Will Nash's *Goin' Down That Long Long Lonesome Road* **includes a four measure intro extended by a two measure "vamp". The two measures of the vamp may be repeated until the singer is ready to come in.**

Vamp till ready

(12 bar)

B'lieve to my soul ___
Woke up this morn -

④ **EASY INTRO**
An __easy intro__ to create is one using the rhythm pattern of the first few measures, or of the whole twelve bar. Play it for two or four measures before beginning the melody.

* ♯5 means the fifth of the "D" chord has been raised 1/2 step (to A♯). This is usually called an augmented chord.

In this arrangement of *The Hesitating Blues,* by W. C. Handy note the introduction of three measures.
How is the melody of this intro related to the song?

THE HESITATING BLUES

W. C. Handy
Arr: U. A. R.

Moderate swing

TURNAROUNDS

Three ways to create a longer blues song:

① Make each of the measures of the twelve bar two measures long instead. This will create 24 measures. Example : *12 Bar Bop,* pg. 36.

② Place a repeat sign at the end of the twelfth bar and play all of the twelve bar over again. Example : *You Got The Color Of Blue,* pg. 53.

③ Connect two twelve bars with a musical bridge, or **turnaround.** Example : *Dallas Blues,* **pg. 44 - 45.**

THE TURNAROUND

A turnaround can be added to a song to connect two different twelve bars; (example A), or be used as a first ending to repeat a twelve bar; (example B).

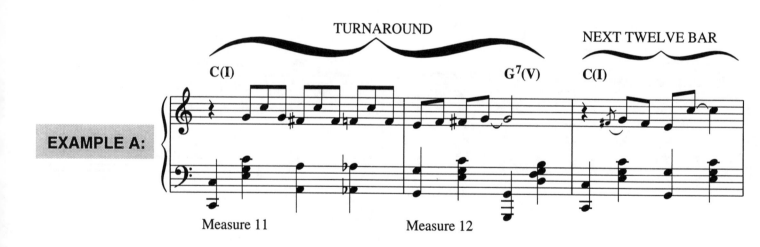

EXAMPLE A:

The last two measures of the twelve bar are used as the turnaround. The aim is to end up on the "V" chord instead of the "I" chord. This alerts the listener to be ready to hear more music. The next twelve bar follows it.

If you want to repeat the same twelve bar after the turnaround, make the last two measures a first ending followed by a repeat sign. For the ending of the second time through, play a different last two measures which sound like a finish.

EXAMPLE B

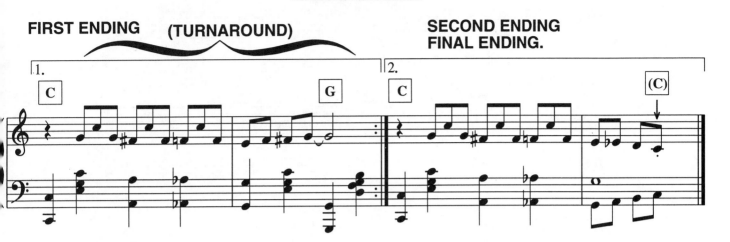

FIRST ENDING   (TURNAROUND)   SECOND ENDING
                                                FINAL ENDING.

Most turnarounds end with a "V" chord. Here are some turnarounds in the key of "C":

CREATE YOUR OWN INTRO AND TURNAROUND

PUT THAT NUMBER ON THE WALL
(AND GIVE THAT MAN A CALL)

U.A.R.
AND: _____

(INTRO.)

FILLS

When the melody of a twelve bar pauses with a rest or held note, such as at the
end of the first or second line, called a "break", you may want to fill in the gap with
a few notes for decoration. Experience and good taste contribute to successful fills.
The following will help you get started.

① **BLUES FILLS**

Example bar 1 and 2

**Examples of blues fills for bars
3 and 4 during held melody note.**

② **CHORD FILL**

Example bar 1 and 2

Examples of chord fills for bars 3 and 4 during rest in the melody. Chord may be blocked (a), or broken (b).

a.

b.

③ **CHROMATIC FILL**

In this example a second line (bars 5 - 8) is shown from the *Tishomingo Blues* by Spencer Williams. The vocal part is written above the piano accompaniment. In measures 7 and 8, when the singer holds the "G" the piano plays a chromatic fill.

Bar 5 - 8 of melody

I want to be where   the win -try winds don't   blow,

Chromatic fill for bars 7 and 8

Joe Turner is one of the oldest known blues songs. It is presented here in "faking" form. Besides adding the left hand style you think fits well, "fill" during the circled measures at the end of line one and two. Create a turnaround (ending in a "V" chord) for the end of the third line.

JOE TURNER

1. They tell me Joe Tur-ner's come and gone _____ They
2. They tell me Joe Tur-ner's come and gone _____ They

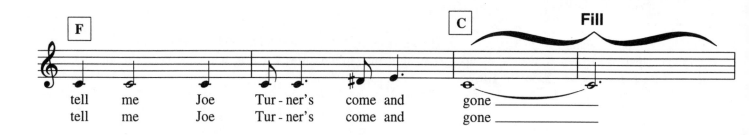

tell me Joe Tur-ner's come and gone _____
tell me Joe Tur-ner's come and gone _____

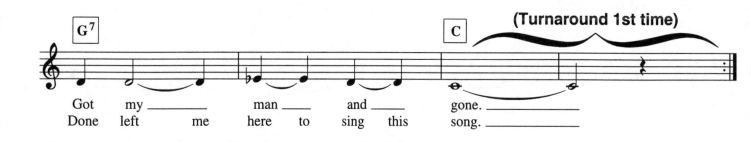

Got my _____ man _____ and _____ gone. _____
Done left me here to sing this song. _____

MINOR BLUES PROGRESSION

A minor chord occurs when the third of a chord (the middle note when in root position) is lowered a half step.

This chord is sometimes heard in the blues. It can be the "I" chord, which creates a blues in a minor key. Using the basic twelve bar pattern for the minor blues, with the lower case numerals representing the minor chords, the three line progression would be:

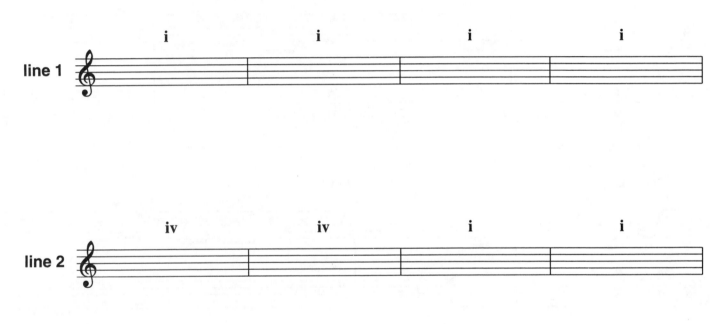

Here's a blues in A minor. The right hand melody is made up of notes from the regular A blues scale.

INSPECTOR BLUE

Moderate swing

U. A. R.

(chromatic . . . .)

* ♭ 5, 7 = A minor chord with the fifth lowered 1/2 step (to E♭). This is usually called a diminished chord.

MORE EXTENDED CHORDS

VOICING 9THS

Extended chords with alternate voicings bring color and excitement to the blues. You can have fun experimenting with these chords when creating your own songs. The examples here will break the surface of regular chords and get you into more sophistocated sounds.

These chords may be used any time you think they fit well. Because they are often in "open inversions" or with the seventh on the bottom, they are served well by a bass player who accompanies with chord foundation notes. When playing solo reach occasionally to a root note down in the bass to help the listener know more easily what chord you're on.

ADDING 9THS:

C⁹ CHORD

C⁹ COMMON VOICING

"OPEN CHORD":

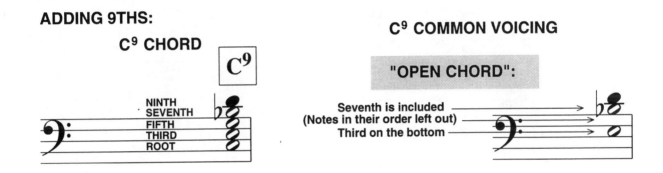

The following are commonly used chords in this voicing. They sound best when played in the octave shown or higher.

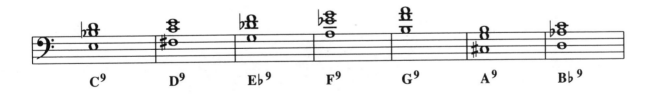

C⁹   D⁹   Eb⁹   F⁹   G⁹   A⁹   Bb⁹

CREATE A SONG WITH 9THS ACCOMPANIMENT

This song has a typical accompainiment of 9th chords. As you form your melody, remember that slow and repeated notes may be easier at first as you coordinate your hands playing together.

TITLE: _____

How you'd like it played: _____

Your name: _____

BORNEO BAY

(A JAZZ WALTZ)

U. A. R.

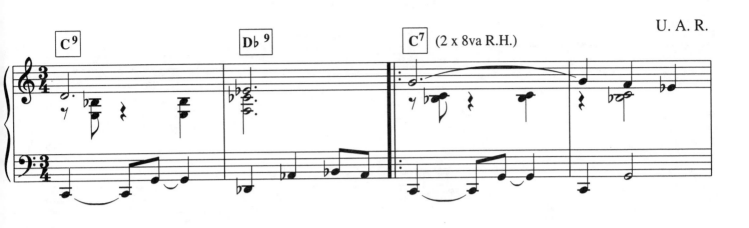

* Chords with 13ths discussed on pg. 77.

76

VOICING 13THS

If we continue to build our chords above the 9th, we add the 11th and the 13th. Even though a chord would be labelled 13th, it can carry the seventh, ninth and eleventh with it. Below is an example of how a C13 chord is formed. The note which is the 13th of a chord is the same note that is often called the 6th of a chord, or the note "A" in a "C" chord.

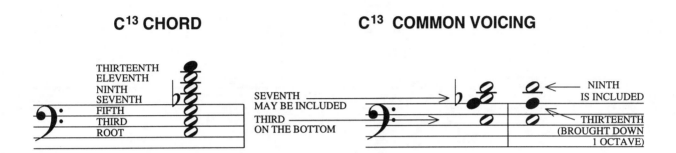

These chords can be used whenever they sound good in a song. Because they are often in inversions and open positions, it is good to occasionally reach down to play the root of the chord. This will help the listener realize what chord you are playing.

Notice how the notes of this chord could easily be interpreted by your ear as either a "Cm^{13}" or an "F^{9}". The difference will be what bass note is given, even if very quickly somewhere during the chord.

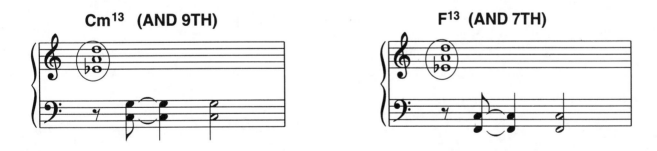

When playing in a blues ensemble, a string bass or electric bass player can supply the root of the chord.

This song contains examples of extended chords, and especially 13th chords. When being sung, the piano would not play all the melody notes along with the singer, just the intro, fills and ending.

I'M THINKIN' OF

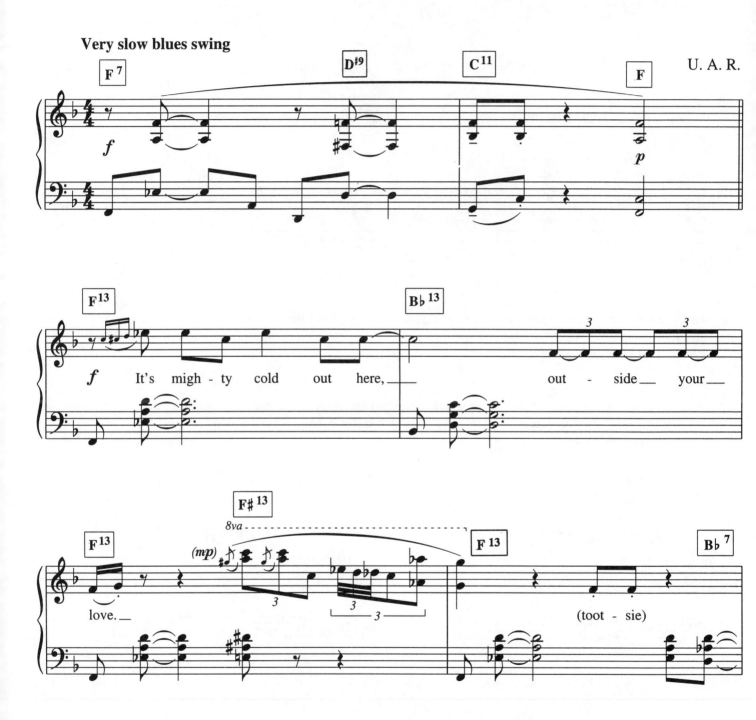

ALTERNATE TWELVE BAR CHORD PATTERNS

The chords in a blues song do not have to follow the traditional twelve bar chord pattern. You have already seen some variations. In the song *The Hesitating Blues* (page 63) there are chords for chromatic color, and a last four bars using a V V I I progression instead of V IV I I.

Below are examples of other possible twelve bar patterns for you to try. They can make your blues sound more interesting and advanced.

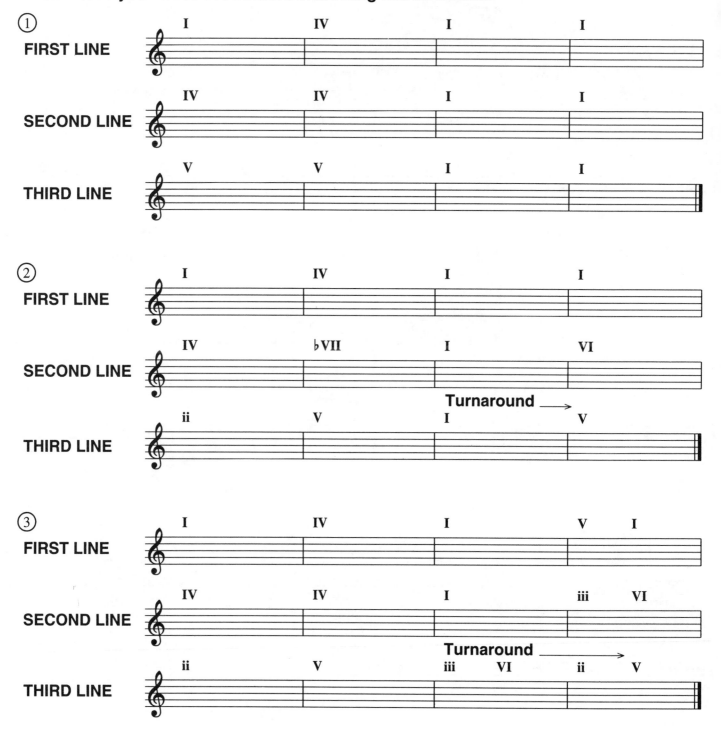

A typical **long form blues song** from the early 20th century will have some variation of the twelve bar progression. Typically it would include an **introduction,** several **verses** and a **chorus.** Using Spencer William's *Tishomingo Blues* (pg. 82) as an example we hear:

     4 **measure introduction**
     2 **measure vamp**
  12 bar blues progression (verse) . . . . ⎱
  32 measure chorus (two 16 bar progressions) ⎰ **This part repeats**

  94 measures (including repeats)

The progression of the twelve bar for Tishomingo Blues is as follows:

(The twelve bar actually begins at m. 7)

TISHOMINGO BLUES

Spencer Williams
Arr. U. A. R.

Line 1

Verse: Oh Mis - si - sip - pi,   Oh Mis - si - sip - pi,   My heart cries out for   you in sad - ness,
To-night I'm pray-in',   To-night I'm say-in',   Oh Lord, please bless the   train that takes me

Line 2

I want to be where   the win - try winds don't   blow, _____
To Tish - o - min - go,   'way down old Dix - ie   way, _____

Line 3

They get you dip-py, with their strange mel-o dies, _____ _____

To re-sist temp-ta-tion, I just can't re-

fuse, _____ In Tish-o-min-go I wish to lin-ger,

Where they play the wea-ry blues. blues. _____

BLUES MONTGOMERY

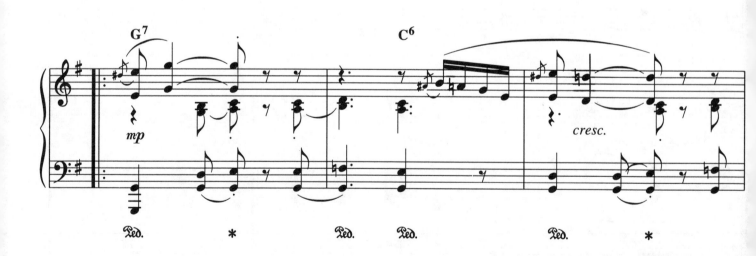

REVIEW OF PART FOUR

1. How long does an introduction have to be?

2. When is a turnaround used in a twelve bar? Why?

3. Name three ways a twelve bar can be made into a longer song.

4. What can you do when a melody line of a twelve bar pauses or rests at the end?

5. How much of a song is given to you when you are expected to fake?

6. How is a minor blues progression different than a regular twelve bar?

7. What other notes can be implied (included) in a 13th chord?

8. How can a half step occur within a 13th voicing?

9. Explain at least two other variations of a twelve bar progression.

10. What changes would you make in your playing of the blues style if you were playing in an ensemble with a bass player? With a singer?

GLOSSARY

GLOSSARY

Basic Blues Scale .... Blues scale without the fourth note. (see: Blues Scale)

Blocked Chord .... Notes of a chord played at the same time.

Blue Notes .... Notes which are a chromatic half step lower than the 3rd, or sometimes 5th, of a major chord.

Blues Scale .... Traditional melodic notes used for blues music. The formula for the six different notes (plus octave) is:

$$\overset{\displaystyle \text{OCTAVE}}{1 \quad 2 \quad 3 \quad 4 \quad 5 \quad 6 \quad 7}$$

$$1\tfrac{1}{2} \quad 1 \quad \tfrac{1}{2} \quad \tfrac{1}{2} \quad 1\tfrac{1}{2} \quad 1$$

Break .... The pause or held note in a melodic line as at the end of line 1 or line 2 in a twelve bar.

Bridge .... A turnaround or transitional section.

Broken Chord .... Notes of a chord played one at a time.

Chord .... Three or more notes designed to be heard with each other.

Chorus .... The section which normally follows the verse in a long form blues song. The words usually stay the same when the music is repeated.

Chromatic .... Next possible adjacent note on the piano, either black or white.

Dominant .... Usually refers to the "V" chord. A dominant seventh chord implies a major chord with an added seventh.

Enharmonics .... Notes which look alike (on the piano), and sound alike, but have different names, i.e. : "C♯" or "D♭".

Ensemble .... A group of two or more people playing music together.

Extended Chord .... What occurs when different notes are added to a three note chord. Usually taken from among notes that would be stacked in thirds above the root position chord.

Fake .... To play a given melody and chord progression while supplying your own left hand pattern and style.

Fill .... Extra notes, not part of the regular melody, played during the break for decoration.

Grace Note .... A note played quickly before another note. It is written as a smaller note than the others around it. Its note value, or length, is taken from the beat before it.

Harmony .... Notes that sound good together, usually from the same chord.

Half Step .... The interval created by moving up or down one chromatic.

Home .... Most important note, or keynote, of a song. The note on which the home chord (chord "I") is based.

Improvise .... To create music "on the spot", or without preparation.

Interval .... The distance between two notes.

Introduction .... Measure or measures used to set a pace and key before the main song begins.

91

Inversion .... Notes of a chord played out of order. When a chord is in first inversion, the 3rd (of the root chord) is at the bottom. In second inversion the 5th is at the bottom.

Key .... The word used to describe which note is "home" in a song. That note implies a particular scale and key signature.

Key Signature .... The resulting ♯'s or ♭'s needed within the I, IV, or V chords of a given home note.

Line .... A four measure segment of the twelve bar progression: line 1 is m. 1-4, line 2 is m. 5-8, etc.

Loco .... A direction to return to the regular location.

Major Chord .... Three notes which follow the formula: 5th $\uparrow$ } 1 $\frac{1}{2}$ steps 3rd $\uparrow$ } 2 steps root $\uparrow$

These same notes may be played out of order, and the chord may be extended.

Melody .... The "tune" or part of a song that would have words. A succession of single notes in a row.

Minor Chord .... Same as a major chord with the 3rd lowered a half step.

Non Chord Tones .... Note used, usually in a melodic line, that is not part of the chord or blues scale in use at that time.

Octave .... The interval of an 8th. Twelve $\frac{1}{2}$ steps above any given note. The note name will be the same.

Pick up .... An incomplete measure to introduce a phrase or song.

Progression .... The order of chords as they change.

Riff .... A short musical idea which, when repeated, can become a musical phrase or be used for a fill.

Root Position .... A chord with its name as the bottom note.

Sub-Dominant .... The chord beginning a 5th below home. The IV chord.

Swing .... The tradition of playing eighth notes unevenly. The eighth note on the beat lasting $\frac{2}{3}$ of the beat, and the eighth note off the beat lasting $\frac{1}{3}$ of the beat.

Transpose .... Translate a phrase or song to a different key.

Turnaround .... What is done at the end of a twelve bar progression so that it can continue on to another twelve bar, or repeat. Usually the last bar or two moves to the V chord instead of remaining on the I chord.

Twelve Bar .... A particular progression of chords within twelve measures. A standard progression is:

I   I   I   I
IV IV I   I
V   IV I   I

Vamp .... Part of a song, usually at the end of an introduction, which repeats as many times as necessary until the soloist is ready to begin.

Voicing .... The arrangements of notes in a chord.

Verse .... The first main section of a long form blues song. It is usually a twelve bar which repeats with different words each time.

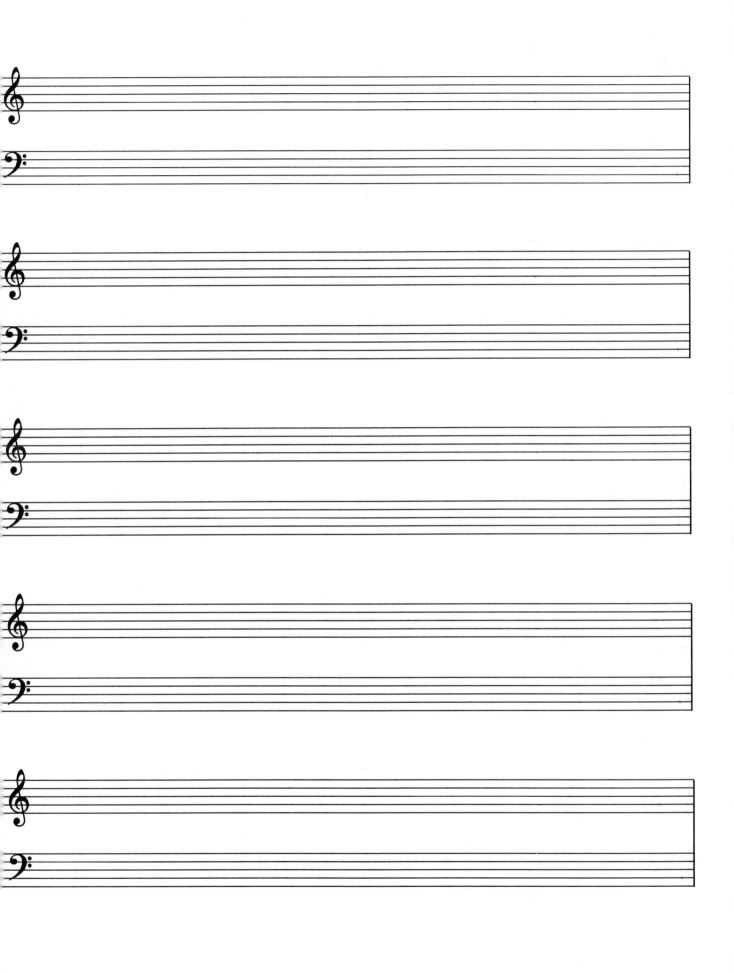

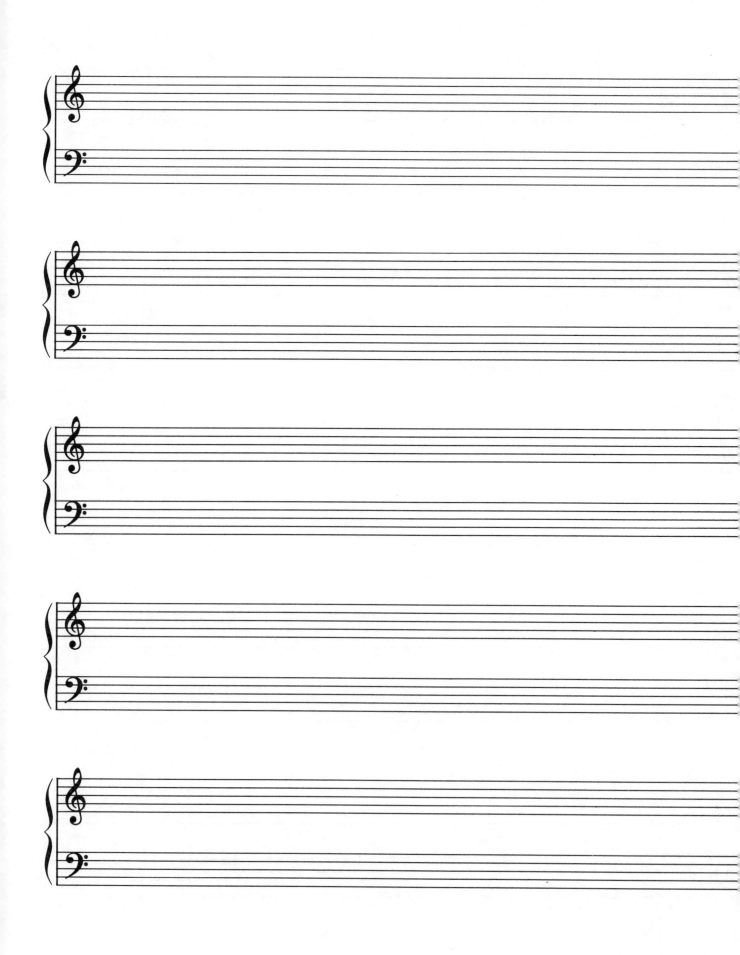